# Working with Animals

## By Hayden Turner and Christopher Cheng

Rigby

# Contents

Introduction                                    3

Cleaning the Animal Shelters   4

In the Kitchen                               6

Feeding Time                               8

The Animal Doctor                   10

Bath Time                                  12

Working at the Zoo              14

Afterword                                  16

# Introduction

My name is Hayden. I'm one of the zoo-keepers at City Zoo.

All the animals in a zoo need food, shelter, and a clean place to live. At City Zoo, we try to give the animals everything they need.

# Cleaning the Animal Shelters

We clean the animal shelters every day. We pick up and hose away the dirt, then put clean sawdust on the floor.

## Did You Know?

The waste from the animal shelters is collected each day. It is recycled and put on to the zoo's gardens.

# In the Kitchen

Each day we chop up fruit, vegetables, and meat for the animals. We weigh the food for each animal and put it in buckets.

Zookeepers make sure the animals have a healthy diet.

We weigh each animal's food to make sure they don't eat too much.

# Did You Know?

A big elephant in the zoo can eat a large bag of carrots, 15 loaves of bread, and lots and lots of hay each day.

# Feeding Time

Food is being "hidden" in this log
for one of the animals to find.

This parrot chick has lost its mother,
so the zookeepers feed it by hand.

Zoo animals like to hunt for their food. Sometimes they find their food in strange places!

Mmm, frozen fish! This bear is breaking open an ice block in search of the frozen fish inside.

## Did You Know?

Sometimes the zoo bears eat fish that are frozen in water. These iceblock fish are called *fishicles*.

# The Animal Doctor

This vet is cleaning dirt out of a leopard's eye.

Animals can get sick, even in a zoo. The vet finds out what makes them sick. Sometimes zookeepers put medicine or vitamins in the animals' food.

Hayden puts medicine in the zebras' food to stop them from getting sick.

To keep seals healthy, vitamin pills are hidden inside their fish dinner.

# Bath Time

Most zoo animals can clean themselves, but sometimes they need our help. Many animals need brushing or combing. Some baby animals even have to be washed in a bath!

Hayden is brushing dust out of the camel's hair.

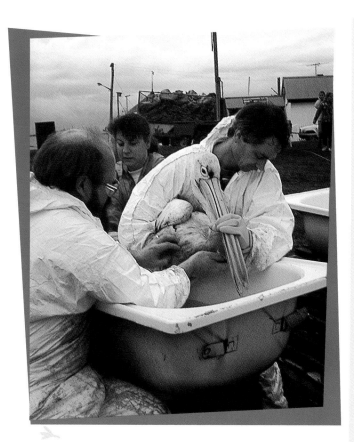

These zookeepers are cleaning a pelican that was coated by oil spilled from a ship.

## Did You Know?

Sometimes zookeepers take home baby animals that don't have a mother. The zookeepers feed and clean the animals.

# Working at the Zoo

Zookeepers work very hard. We are always trying to learn more about the animals we look after. We try to give the animals everything they need.

Hayden is using the Internet to find the latest information about animals.

Hayden and John are always looking for ways to improve the zoo.

# Did You Know?

In the past, zoos kept animals behind bars. But now their homes in the zoo look like they do in the wild.

# Afterword

I love animals, and I always have. When I was a boy, my friends had puppies and kittens as pets. But I was different—my first pet was a chicken!

I have always loved being surrounded by animals, so being a zookeeper is my ideal job.

When I'm on vacation, I visit zoos in other countries. My favorite place in the world is Africa, because of its amazing animals.

*Hayden*